WILDERNESS ADVENTURES

Canoeing and Kayaking

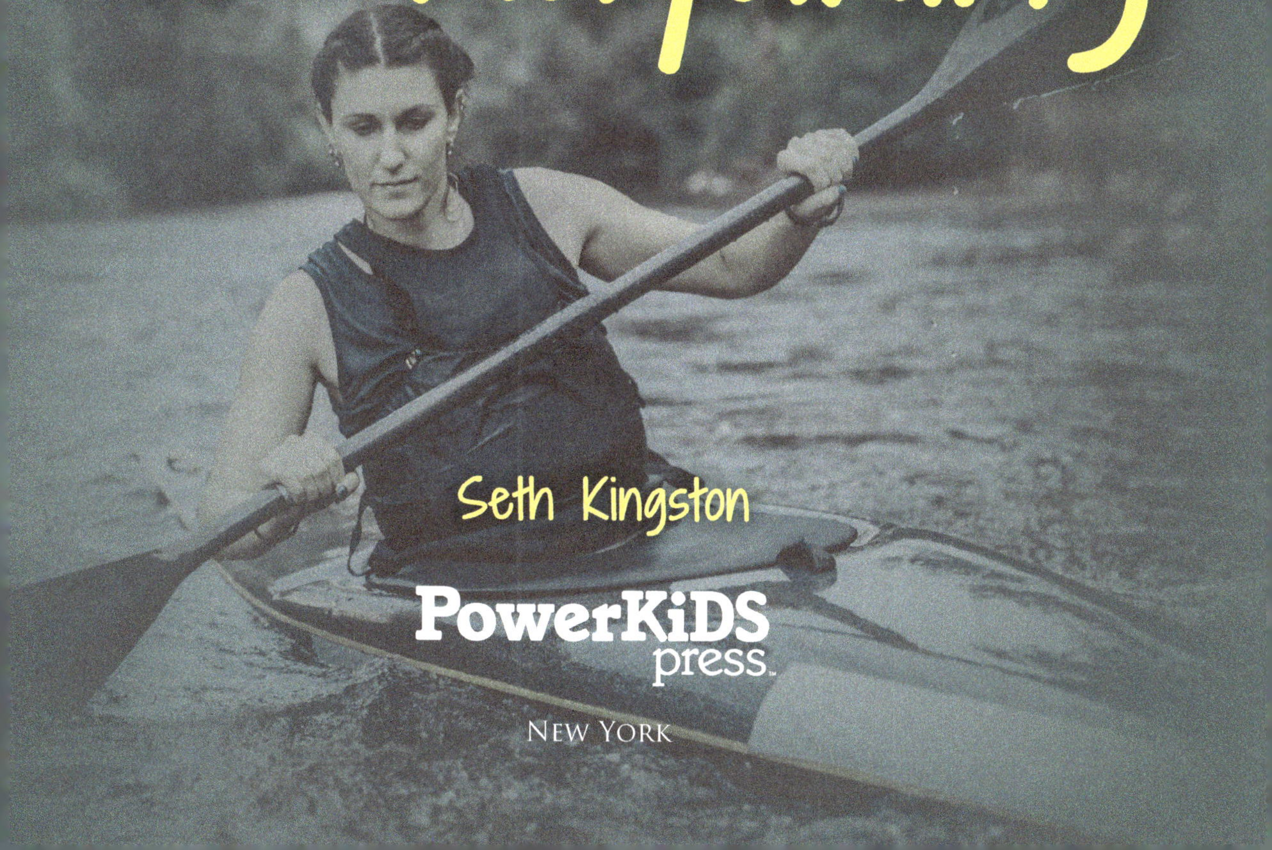

Seth Kingston

PowerKiDS press.

New York

Published in 2022 by The Rosen Publishing Group, Inc.
29 East 21st Street, New York, NY 10010

First Edition

Portions of this work were originally authored by Suzanne Slade and published as *Let's Go Canoeing and Kayaking*. All new material in this edition was authored by Seth Kingston.

Editor: Caitie McAneney
Book Design: Michael Flynn

Photo Credits: Cover (kayaker) South_agency/E+/Serbia/Getty Images; cover, pp. 7, 13, 17, 29 (mountain logo) doyz86/Shutterstock.com; interior (mountain background) Lidiia/Shutterstock.com; p. 4 kali9/E+/Getty Images; p. 5 PetrBonek/iStock/Getty Images; p. 7 Hulton Archive/Hulton Fine Art Collection/Getty Images; p. 9 Ariel Skelley/DigitalVision/Getty Images; p. 10 LazarPhotography/iStock/Getty Images; p. 11 Ascent/PKS Media Inc/Stone/Getty Images; p. 13 D. Pimborough/Shutterstock.com; p. 15 mysticenergy/iStock/Getty Images; p. 17 Mike Powell/DigitalVision/Getty Images; p. 19 Wolfgang Kaehler/LightRocket/Getty Images; p. 20 edelmar/iStock/Getty Images; p. 21 Chanintorn Vanichsawangphan/EyeEm/Getty Images; p. 23 Matthäus Rojek/iStock/Getty Images; p. 24 Comstock Images/Stockbyte/Getty Images; p. 25 Corbis/VCG/Corbis/Getty Images; p. 27 sturti/E+/Getty Images; p. 29 Boone Rodriguez/Corbis/VCG/Corbis/Getty Images.

Library of Congress Cataloging-in-Publication Data

Names: Kingston, Seth, author.
Title: Canoeing and kayaking / Seth Kingston.
Description: New York, NY : PowerKids Press, [2022] | Series: Wilderness adventures | Includes index.
Identifiers: LCCN 2020039415 | ISBN 9781725329270 (library binding) | ISBN 9781725329256 (paperback) | ISBN 9781725329263 (6 pack)
Subjects: LCSH: Canoes and canoeing Juvenile literature. | Kayaking--Juvenile literature.
Classification: LCC GV784.3 .K56 2022 | DDC 797.122--dc23
LC record available at https://lccn.loc.gov/2020039415

Manufactured in the United States of America

Some of the images in this book illustrate individuals who are models. The depictions do not imply actual situations or events.

Note to Parents and Teachers: Some of the activities in this book require adult supervision. Please talk with your child or student before allowing them to proceed with any wilderness activities.

CPSIA Compliance Information: Batch #CWPK22. For further information contact Rosen Publishing, New York, New York at 1-800-237-9932.

CONTENTS

Fun on the Water

Do you love spending time on the water? You don't have to stay on the shore. You can try canoeing and kayaking! Canoeing and kayaking are fun water sports that can be done alone or with a big group of people. It's important to follow safety rules though, like wearing a life jacket and having adult **supervision**.

Canoeing and kayaking are great ways to exercise, relax, and explore. You can paddle down a winding river or glide across a glassy lake. You can learn about animals in the water and discover new kinds of fish. You can observe animals on nearby land or spot the ducks and geese that swim by. There's so much to see and do out on the water.

WILD FILE

Some people consider kayaks to be a kind of canoe. They are different in many ways, including shape and paddle design.

Canoeing and kayaking can be fun activities for all ages.

Canoes Throughout History

Peoples around the world have been using **watercraft**, like canoes, for thousands of years. They used what was available, including logs, bark, and animal skins. Canoes were used for transportation and trade, and sometimes fighting. One of the oldest canoes ever found was the Pesse Canoe in today's Netherlands, which may be around 10,000 years old!

Early Native Americans made different kinds of canoes using different materials. Peoples of the Pacific Northwest used western red cedar trees to create solid, one-piece canoes called dugout canoes, some with sails. Native peoples in the Northeast used bark from birch trees for their canoes. Peoples living in the Arctic used walrus skins on their canoes. Smaller canoes were used for short fishing trips, while larger canoes could carry many people during war.

CHEROKEE DUGOUT CANOES

Dugout canoes were used by several groups of native peoples in the Americas. Each group had used their own materials and designs. The Cherokee often used hardwood. First, they had to find a huge log, sometimes up to 40 feet (12.2 m) long. They cut down the tree and hollowed it using a combination of fire and hand tools. They used bear fat to make the canoe waterproof.

This artwork from the 1700s shows native peoples in the Yosemite Valley using dugout canoes.

Canoe How-To

Today, you can buy or rent canoes just for fun. Canoes usually fit more people than kayaks because they have open decks. Usually, there are one or two seats for paddlers to sit on, so canoes often hold one to four people.

One person sits at the stern, or back, of the boat. A second person can sit at the canoe's bow, or front. The people in the bow and stern do the paddling. Passengers often sit on the floor in the middle of the canoe.

You don't want to get caught up a river without a paddle! Paddles help **propel** and direct your canoe. To hold your paddle, grab the shaft, or pole, with one hand and grip the top with the other. The blade of the paddle will go in the water.

WILD FILE

The bottom of a canoe is called a hull. You can sit or store your gear in the hull as you fish.

It's easy to tip a canoe! Keep still when possible. When you have to get in and out, keep your weight in the center of the boat.

Different Strokes

It's important to learn how to paddle before you hit the water. If two people are paddling a canoe, the person at the stern does the steering. The person in the bow often sets the pace, or speed, of the paddling.

There are three basic paddling strokes. To move forward, place the entire blade of the paddle in the water at a right angle to the canoe. Pull back on the paddle while keeping it close beside the boat. To move sideways, turn the paddle blade so it faces you. Place the paddle out in the water as far as you can and pull it toward you. A C-shaped stroke to the left will turn the canoes right. A C-shaped stroke to the right will turn the canoe left.

WILD FILE

Are you rowing your canoe alone? Solo paddlers sit at the stern, or back, of the canoe.

Practice different strokes as you start out on your canoeing adventure. You'll get the hang of it soon enough!

Extreme Canoeing!

If you're looking for an **extreme** canoeing challenge, you might want to try white-water canoeing. This exciting sport involves canoeing over fast-moving water.

You need special training, skills, and gear before you can go white-water canoeing. Helmets and life jackets are must-have gear for this high-speed activity. Wearing goggles and a rain jacket can protect you from the spray of crashing waves. Many people white-water canoe with a guide. They can help you learn to "read" a river, or be able to spot signs of danger in the water ahead. You need to steer quickly around large rocks and fallen trees on a white-water course. As with any extreme sport, it's important to have adult supervision and to learn safety rules before you hit the water.

WHITE-WATER PARKS

Where can you find a fun and challenging white-water course? You can go to a white-water park! The U.S. Whitewater Center in Charlotte, North Carolina, is home to the world's largest man-made **recirculating** white-water river. It has white-water rapids and channels for kayaks and canoes. Many white-water parks have different levels, from beginner to **expert**. These are great places for white-water racers to practice their downhill skills.

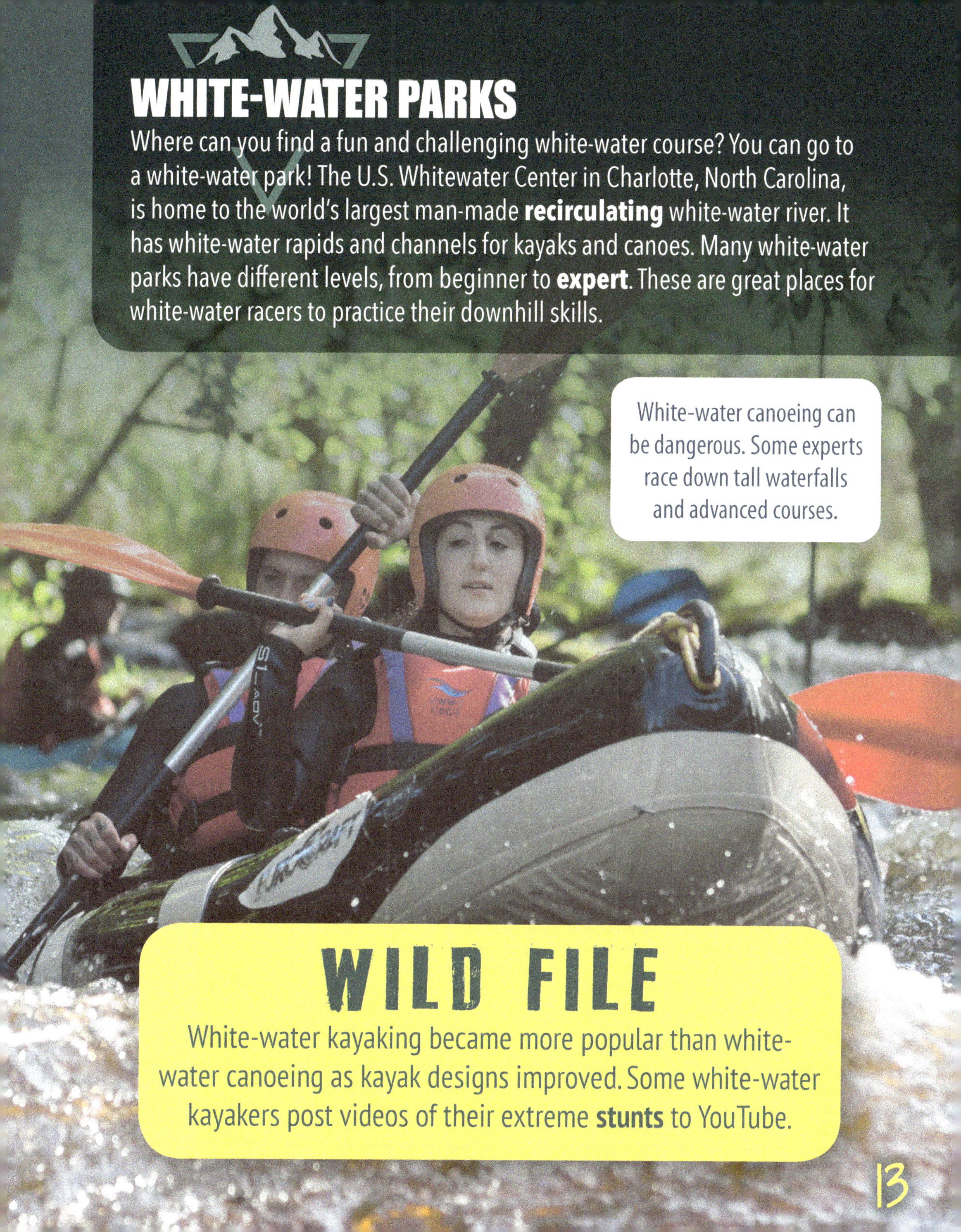

White-water canoeing can be dangerous. Some experts race down tall waterfalls and advanced courses.

WILD FILE

White-water kayaking became more popular than white-water canoeing as kayak designs improved. Some white-water kayakers post videos of their extreme **stunts** to YouTube.

Camp with Canoes!

Some canoe trips last a few hours. Others can last a few days. You can pack everything you need to camp out along a river. As you drift down a river, you can set up camp in a different place each night.

You have to pack light, since you'll carry everything in your canoe. Pack a tent, food, sleeping bags, pillows, bug spray, matches, and dry clothing for camping. When you find your camping spot, tie up your canoe securely with a rope or pull it up on the shore. Choose a flat, dry location to pitch your tent. If you want to start a campfire, find a safe place far from trees or dry plants. Cook your meal over the fire and get ready for a new day of canoeing!

WILD FILE

If something blocks your path on a river trip, such as a fallen tree or dam, you can portage. Portaging is when you carry your canoe across land.

Canoe camping allows you to wake up to a view unlike any other.

Spot the Differences

Can you spot the differences between a kayak and a canoe? Like a canoe, a kayak has a hull on bottom, but it also has a deck on top. Sit-in kayaks have one or two holes, called cockpits, in the deck. One passenger sits in each cockpit. In cold or choppy waters, kayakers might wear a spray skirt to keep dry. It fits around the kayaker's waist and fastens to the kayak. If you don't mind getting wet, you might also try a sit-on-top kayak.

How can you direct your kayak? A rudder, or skeg, is a part that dips into the water at the stern (back) of some kayaks. It can keep you on track. As with a canoe, your most important tool is your paddle!

WILD FILE

Some kayaks have a hard shell, while others are inflatable. Inflatable kayaks are easier to transport, because you can let the air out and roll them up.

HOW TO PADDLE A KAYAK

A kayak paddle has two blades. First, you have to grip it correctly. Put the paddle over your head. Adjust your hands so your elbows are at right (or 90 degree) angles. Then, bring the paddle in front of you. To go forward, put a blade in the water near your foot and pull back. Keep doing that side to side. To go backward, put a blade in the water near your hip, and push forward.

These kayakers have spray skirts to keep dry while they're on the water.

Creating the Kayak

Different forms of canoe have been used around the world for thousands of years. However, kayaks were first used for colder, northern climates. Kayaks were probably first used in Greenland by Eskimo peoples (sometimes called Inuit). Eskimo refers to indigenous peoples of northern Canada, Greenland, eastern Siberia, and Alaska. Kayaks were important for transportation and also hunting seals and fishing.

While some canoes could carry many people, kayaks were designed to usually carry only one person at a time. The frame was covered with animal skins to keep the icy Arctic waters out. Some had frames made of driftwood, while others used whale bones. They were sometimes covered in whale fat for waterproofing. Kayaking for fun started in Europe in the mid-1800s, and it was featured as an Olympic sport in 1936.

Kayaks have changed over the years, but many important features come from traditional kayak designs.

Kayaking on the Sea

Sea kayaking can open you up to new waters, new views, and new challenges. Sea kayaks aren't as deep as regular kayaks. Their shallow bodies allow them to move in close to shore. They are also longer and thinner than other kinds of kayaks. This long, sleek boat travels quietly through the water. You can use a sea kayak to get near birds and animals in the ocean.

Some people surf large ocean waves with kayaks. To catch a ride on the wave, the kayaker must paddle quickly when it approaches.

Some people like to take their sea kayaks on long trips. The front of a sea kayak has several hatches, where food, water, clothing, or a small tent can be stored. It's important to watch the weather when you go sea kayaking. You don't want to be caught in open waters during a storm.

You can kayak in ocean waters in both tropical climates and cold climates.

Up Close with Nature

Whether you've chosen a canoe or kayak for your adventure, you have the ability to get up close with nature. You can observe many types of animals while boating, both in the water and on shore. Canoes and kayaks allow you to go into shallow waters, where larger boats can't go. These small boats are powered by people instead of engines. This makes them quiet. You can approach animals without scaring them.

Listen for the calls of different birds while you are drifting down a river. Watch for turtles poking their heads above the water for air or frogs resting on the shore. If you look closely, you might see fish swimming under the water's surface. You can bring a **water-resistant** camera to take pictures of the animals and plants you find.

WILD FILE

Canoes and kayaks don't use fuel, so they don't pollute. Also, unlike boats with fast-moving blades, they're less likely to hurt animals in the water.

Always respect nature when you're kayaking or canoeing. Don't get *too* close to wild animals. Observe them from a safe distance.

Making Plans

Where would you like to take your kayak or canoe? It's a good idea to make a plan before your trip. You might have a lake, river, or pond near you. Look for signs that **indicate** a place is safe for public kayaking or canoeing. You should avoid private waters or unsafe areas. Many public lakes and rivers have a ramp where you can **launch** a boat. Some launching areas charge a small fee to put your boat in the water.

If you're an experienced kayaker or canoer and you want a challenge, you might want to check out faster-moving waters. If you're new to the sport, a quiet pond is the perfect place to relax and practice your new skills.

Many state and national parks rent kayaks and canoes for people who don't have their own. They also have areas that are **designated** for safe water sports.

What Should You Pack?

Once you choose a location for your trip and know how long it will last, you can start to pack everything you'll need. The right gear will help you have a smooth and safe trip. The most important thing you will need is a life jacket. Every person in the boat should wear a properly fitting life jacket. You should also bring a hat and sunscreen.

On cool days, pack dry clothes and a jacket in case you get wet. On hot days, pack a swimsuit so you can cool off in the water. Pack a fishing pole if you want to catch fish. For longer canoe or kayak trips, you'll have to pack supplies like extra clothes, food, and a tent.

Paddling a kayak or canoe is hard work! Pack plenty of food and water for your trip.

Time to Explore

Do you think you'd prefer a canoe? These boats are quite stable and can usually fit more people. Or would you rather use a kayak to get around? These boats are often faster. Kayaks and canoes are great watercraft for exploring ponds, lakes, and rivers. Some people just want to relax and fish on calm waters. Others try extreme sports like white-water canoeing or surf kayaking.

Wherever you choose to canoe or kayak, take time to enjoy nature. You can't beat the smell of fresh air and the sound of water lapping against your boat. Follow safety rules and always have adult supervision, especially when you're a beginner. Plan your trip, pack up your gear, and it's time to hit the water!

Explore the waterways around you. There are endless opportunities for adventure!

SAFETY TIPS

- Always canoe or kayak with adult supervision.
- Wear a life jacket that fits you every time you go out on the water.
- Look for signs that say if an area is safe for water sports and open to the public.
- Sit as still as possible in your canoe or kayak to keep your balance.
- Practice "rolling" techniques on your kayak with adult supervision so you know how to deal with righting yourself if you flip in the water.
- Keep away from water that is moving too quickly or seems shallow and rocky.
- Pack lots of water and food while you're out on the water.

GLOSSARY

designated: Set apart for a specific purpose.

expert: Someone who knows a great deal about something.

extreme: Very great in degree.

indicate: To be a sign of something; to state something.

launch: To set a boat or ship afloat.

propel: To push something forward.

recirculate: To move in a circle over and over.

stunt: An unusual or difficult activity that requires great skill or daring.

supervision: The act of watching and directing what someone does or how something is done.

watercraft: Something used for water transport, such as a boat.

water-resistant: Able to keep water out.

FOR MORE INFORMATION

Books

Palmer, Andrea. *We're Going Freshwater Fishing*. New York, NY: PowerKids Press, 2017.

Siegel, Rebecca. *Rivers and Streams!: With 25 Science Projects for Kids*. White River Junction, VT: Nomad Press, 2018.

Websites

Canoe Facts for Kids
kids.kiddle.co/Canoe
Learn more about canoes on this kid-friendly site.

The Inuit
firstpeoplesofcanada.com/fp_groups/fp_inuit4.html
Learn more about the Inuit—indigenous peoples of northern Canada—and how they developed kayaks for fishing.

INDEX